Girl, Interrupted

Ayanna Stevens

BookLeaf
Publishing

Presentation by *BookLeaf Publishing*

Web: www.bookleafpub.com

E-mail: info@bookleafpub.com

ISBN: 9789395969277

First edition 2022

DEDICATION

I dedicate this book to the younger versions of myself that could not see, feel or believe in who she was. I also dedicate this book to every person who has struggled to find the words or confidence to express themselves.

This is for you. Love Ay x

ACKNOWLEDGEMENT

For might art Thou, praised and glorious,
and to Thee be glory, world without end.

Amen

PREFACE

'My mission in life is to not only survive, but to thrive; and to do so with some passion, some compassion, some humour, and some style.'

Maya Angelou

one

Call me Autumn.
Like the season.
My nights aren't the darkest.
Call me change.
Call me harvest.
Wearing truth.
Bearing fruit.
My Days hold out.
Sunlight warms the skin.
New feelings.
Cool breezes.
Call me transition.
New day.
New positions.
Adjusting.
New admissions.
Nobody will notice.
Try something new.
Pray more.
Hope less.
Don't stress.
Other side of winter.
But know this.
Still the closest thing to summer.
Humbled in the centre.
There's nothing new without this season.
Set your intentions.
Like a call before you enter.
It's Autumn.

two

Travelling
Moving
Different directions
Diversions and traffic
Intersections
Journey in grace
Regardless
Be heart led
Affirming your faith
Set pace
Sensibly
Build your endurance
Built for performance
Raise stakes
Take chances
Calculate your risk
No martyrs
Just dedicated travellers
Movers
Moving in different directions
Towards the same destination.

three

Let's stay close.
Connected.
Connections,
I work best with.
Collisions.
Colliding.
Sliding doors.
I need impact.
Resonance.
Reciprocity.
Reverence.
Intact.
I need energy.
Therapy.
Masking's a felony.
Let's stay close.
Connected.
We need
connections.

four

Flight mode.
Prepare for take off.
Prepare for brakes off.
Prepare for moments of
Silence,
Steadiness,
Soaring.
Prepare to rise above,
falling.
Prepare for new sights.
New heights.
Prepare for resistance.
Drag.
Unnecessary weight.
Bags.
Prepare to lighten the load.
Brighten the soul.
Block distractions.
Lucid actions.
Prepare for the inevitable.
At all costs,
Be prepared.
All loss…
Lessons disguised.
We're in flight.
Up up and awaiting.
Just stay prepared.

five

Water signs
take me to the ocean.
Sandy shores.
Lands end.
Deepest blues.
Widest open.
Calm seas don't…
you know…
Still choppy waves,
bad omens.
Showmen.
Wild on the surface
but deep dive
and you'll know them.
Murky waters.
Obscured vision.
Right before my eyes,
but I keep vision in mind.
Flow with the tide.
Swim good
I can ocean dive.
I'm only shallow on purpose.
Only shallow needs perfect,
imperfections are more my type.
No two waves the same,
I adore my sign.
Unpredictable.

Comfortably.
Ebbs and flows,
current under me.
Touch the shore
for a moment
then back to sea.
I can't keep it shallow.
No stagnant pond.
Natural bonds.
Take cues from the elements,
Nature's songs.
I zone out to the sounds of the waves.
Natural's home.
I rest easy.
Drifting,
Floating,
To deep sleep.
Best you release me.
Who's hoping?
That's weak knees
I wage bets
in the deep sea.
High tide
at full moon.
I'm a learner
Teach me.
Or leave please.
It's low tide at sunrise,
You can paddle in seaweed,
or watch from shore.
Every wave wants more,
so we roll on...

regardless.
That's the hard line.
No love lost.
The heart line.
Absentees get discarded,
tossed out with the tide.
I know that sounds heartless...
but the ocean takes no prisoners,
knows no bounds.
It's in those depths,
that truth can be found.

six

I went in search of the sunset.
The pinks and purples.
Peach skies.
Been holding my breath since the sunrise.
I went in search of relief.
The ambers and oranges.
Shades that speak to me
& for me.
I didn't find the sunset.
It happened,
I just missed it.
Wrong direction.
Poor timing.
Instead I stumbled upon the night.
Not quite stillness,
but slower.
Saw the light change to darkness
and discovered,
that what I found
was what I needed.

seven

The
beauty
and
brilliance
of
bottling
it
all
in
is
found
in
the
relief
and
respite
of
the
release.

Just don't hold it for too long.

eight

Lost for words...
worked so hard in the search...
but I remain calm
because I've learnt...
...I'm learning
that sometimes
silence works
and we can find peace in the worst.
Discernment.
Discerning
these loud thoughts
aren't whispers.
Definitely
deafening.
Do you hear it?
Need to say everything.
Fearlessly
caring
'Till I can't say anything.
I'm here less...
Honestly
Not planning for more visits.
I fear rest.
Actively engaging
in this presence
is powerful
and still...

I'm Lost for words.
Though I worked so hard in the search
Still I remain calm
because I've learnt...
...I'm learning
that sometimes
silence works
and we can find peace in the worst...
...of it all

nine

Let's keep it PC
Sadness is relative
Joy's cousin
Peace is needed
Calm is a sedative
Opposite of negative
We avoid judging
Optimism… imperative
But judgements in everything
Let's speak openly
I'm imperfect
Acknowledgement
Brings me peace
I'll fall apart and pick up the pieces
No pity needed
Don't avoid subjects
Therapy is what we need,
Whatever the form
And pace
Does not mean speed
But move on it
Pace does not mean freeze
It's PC
Meaning peaceful calm
Because if not
It's up in arms
Proper carnage

So I'm armoured
Full metal chest plate
To guard my heart
And restart it
Pulmonary circuit
For those asking
It's been
Properly considered
I'm perfectly capable
Of owning my decisions
Owning my ambitions
And remaining
Perfectly calm

ten

Some of us
see angels
Spirit filled
Life force limitless
Raised vibrations
I closed my eyes
and saw you
Your energy
filled the room
I could feel you
in everything
Everywhere
Overwhelming but
Beautiful
Supernatural
I don't believe in magic
or chance
But I believe that
some of us have angels
Who remain close
And can be found
Even amidst the
background noise
and racing thoughts
Even outside of
silent contemplation
And prayer
With us
and within us
All the time

eleven

Readiness
I'm ready to begin
Ready for anything
Ready for a brand new day
Like dawn darkness
Ready is an advantage
Life's journey presents
Twist and turns
Ready is adaptable
Not inflexible or rigid
Like cartilage
Bend too far and break
Ready can counter the carnage
Stay ready for it all
Who created our limits?
My mind decides most things
Who stays… What wins
We often pick our defeats
If we're honest
Being ready
holds me accountable
On my best day
I'd rather lose it all
Than be countable
No commodity
More oddity
I'm allowed to fall
Down, back, behind

My bounce backs
Are divine
Lands me on clouds
Nine
Journey into mind
Ready for that?
No more floating in denial
Did that already
Plus I have an allergy to lies
I choose life
Direct
I choose live
With all of its action
I'll be ready for it
In and out of cameras and lights
Dark nights are always
followed by the sunrise
So I stay ready

twelve

I no longer check
the forecast,
Prepared for any weather,
Pack a coat,
Something waterproof,
Got shades
and an umbrella,
I'm not checking for the storm clouds,
Not quite dancing in the rain,
Not afraid to get my face wet,
Keep it moving all the same,
Plus I have a thing for rainbows,
Pretty colours cut the plain,
If it blows I'll put my hood up,
Gale force winds can't stop my day,
I love waking up to snowfall,
Something warm about those days,
When it's cold we have to wrap up
extra warm to compensate,
It's just funny how in summer,
Everybody will complain,
About the same hot weather,
Missing when the seasons change,
I don't really like the darkness,
Warmth and sunlight keeps me sane,
I've found sunshine in some people,
They glow brighter than the rays,
I've found rain to be refreshing,

I've found cold can clear the mind,
I've found checking for the forecast now
Is just a waste of time,
Stay prepared for any weather,
It's all out of our control,
I know how I feel is up to me,
Not grey skies,rain, or snow.

thirteen

Sometimes
words fail us,
We say it best
with the look in our eyes,
Gentle touch,
Laced fingers.
With an embrace,
Squeezing tight,
Deepening sighs.
Sometimes,
a smile can tell it all.
Answer unasked questions,
Reassurance,
Encouragement,
Validation.
Sometimes all we really need,
is to not say a word.
Listen to what isn't being said
but is being shown.
We're multilingual.
Without words or phrases,
talk to me
in a way I can feel.
Built in translators.
I won't miss a thing
or misunderstand.
Don't hold back.
Hold me close.
Hold me down.

fourteen

Over tired
Under stimulated
Meetings with my head
I need a break
But I have obligations
Privileges
I'm blessed to serve
And showing up
That's not debated
Tuesday's child is full of Grace
But on this day
I prayed for patience
Eased the stress
To show I'm favoured
Grateful
I have sight
Perspective
I'm at home
At every station
Wednesday's child is full of woe
But present tense
Means not relating
I'm ok plus
I can keep eyes off the pavement
Time's a healer
Love's the sweetest fragrance
Everything I give
Will be returned
100 fold
Just waiting

fifteen

Birds of a feather
Fly in formation
It fascinates me
Have you seen
The way they soar?
So coordinated
Togetherness is powerful
Beautiful
Too underrated
Flock together
Believers
Stay close to nature
They better
understand the assignment
Written in his second letter
Protect, trust, hope, persevere
Always
See that in the skies
Not always present in real life
But if you rise
at dawn and listen
Watch the magic at the sun's rise
Or observe the sky at dusk
You'll see what's written
there
Intentionally
In their movements
and their songs
Aves on a mission
On job
On assignment

Pursuit and function strong
Perfectly designed
Since the 5th day
If I could fly above the Earth
I'd have a better view
of time
of life
of minds
We can't see it at sea level
The aerial view's divine
Like a magnifier
Smaller but clearer
Amazed by His creation
Respect it from
respectful distance
That means Semi-fearful
Only because
it goes beyond
what I can humanly imagine
Cannot be fathomed
Without further study
I just feel like
The sky is where you find true freedom
So I look towards it
Learn from it
Try to emulate
it's unconfined limits
The sky is the bench mark
Soaring above - the view
The birds are love and freedom
and their song are songs of truth

sixteen

I'm all alone
Uncommunicative
Speaking to myself
That doesn't count
I'm feeling stressed
& anxious thoughts
mean breathing deep for balance
Racing minds
Chasing peace & quiet
Calm can't be established
I need help
But I can't waste my time
So I just speak in silence

seventeen

I realise
I require
Different things
That most people
Don't naturally
possess.
Politely
unconfine me.
I have phobias.
Tight spaces.
Locked doors.
I need room.
Space and air
to breathe.
I realise that
What I need
Cannot be
guessed.
Is probably
deemed
difficult.
Unreasonable.
I realise to be
Unlike
everyone else,
Means to do
most things
differently

and requiring
extraordinary
things
from people
Who only
have experience
in ordinary.

eighteen

Dear Love,

I apologise,
I should treat you better,
Know I need you.
You believe me?
I'll have hand on heart forever,
It's just lately,
Feeling changes
I'm not sure how much I know you.
Given time
and feel it's running out.
I'm open,
Watch me show you.
But it's different.
That's not insecure,
I feel it
Anti-social
Anti-owe you anything
I'm holding everything I go through.
You can't help me,
Every time it feels the same,
Too late for told you so's,
I'll hold you close,
and you'll act glad I came,
The empty overdose
is strange.

Actually... forget I said anything,

nineteen

I've watched you grow
Watched you sleep
Watched you play
Watched you close
I've watched you hurt
Watched you wonder
Watched you watching me
And I've observed
His greatest favour
Unquantifiable blessings
Irreplaceable gifts
Unteachable lessons
I'm so eternally and entirely
Full
And great
And grateful
Because of you both

twenty

Sometimes
At the end of it all
Just take a moment
And be grateful

twenty-one

These words are overdue
I hope they speak to you
You're growing well
Your aura, smile and
Your innocence
is beautiful
I'm proud of you
Eventually you'll feel it for yourself
You'll learn to manage all your gifts
You'll grow
Investing in your health
Your Will is strong
Your heart is rich
Don't Overcompensate for wealth
And people see what you possess
They'll hold you.
Best you hold yourself
Hearts are pure
but so is trauma
You won't feel at peace in drama
You won't realise when you've made it
Life's a gift and so is karma
Keep on fighting
Locks will open
Guard the parts
you know can break
Work on healing
Peel the plasters

Keep on seeking
Sight is great
And When it's real
you will feel it
Trust what intuition says
You thought you walked alone
Been footsteps all along the way
Stay honest
Stay brave
Seek knowledge
And pray
Stay unique
Never change
Wish you'd heard this everyday

www.ingramcontent.com/pod-product-compliance
Lightning Source LLC
La Vergne TN
LVHW010934200726

843509LV00013B/2220